JIM LIMBER DAVIS
A Black Orphan in the
Confederate
WHITE HOUSE

JIM LIMBER DAVIS
A Black Orphan in the
Confederate
WHITE HOUSE

By Rickey Pittman

Illustrated by Judith Hierstein

PELICAN PUBLISHING COMPANY

GRETNA 2007

To the lost and forgotten children of the Confederacy.
It is your story I wanted to tell. —R. P.

The word "Pelican" and the depiction of a pelican are
trademarks of Pelican Publishing Company, Inc., and
are registered in the U.S. Patent and Trademark Office.

Library of Congress Cataloging-in-Publication Data

Pittman, Rickey.
  Jim Limber Davis : a Black orphan in the Confederate White
House / by Rickey Pittman ; illustrated by Judith Hierstein.
       p. cm.
  Audience: Grades K-3.
  ISBN 978-1-58980-435-7 (hardcover : alk. paper)
  1. Davis, Jim Limber—Juvenile literature. 2. Davis, Jefferson,
1808-1889—Family—Juvenile literature. 3. African American
boys—Virginia—Richmond—Biography—Juvenile literature. 4.
Free African Americans—Virginia—Richmond—Biography—
Juvenile literature. 5. Orphans—Virginia—Richmond—
Biography—Juvenile literature. 6. Adopted children—Virginia—
Richmond—Biography—Juvenile literature. 7. Richmond (Va.)—
Biography—Juvenile literature. 8. Richmond (Va.)—History—
Civil War, 1861-1865—Juvenile literature. 9. United States—
History—Civil War, 1861-1865—Juvenile literature. I. Hierstein,
Judy, ill. II. Title.
  E467.1.D26P48 2007
  973.7'13092—dc22
  [B]

                                        2006036282

Printed in China
Published by Pelican Publishing Company, Inc.
1000 Burmaster Street, Gretna, Louisiana 70053

Jim Limber Davis:
A Black Orphan in the
Confederate White House

Jim Limber was only five years old when his mother and father died from fever and he was placed in the care of a relative in Richmond. Jim's guardian was a cruel man. He often whipped Jim for the smallest mistakes and sent him to bed without supper. Sometimes Jim was so cold, hungry, and sad that he would cry himself to sleep.

One night Jim whispered, "Mama, I miss you. Jim's got it real hard now. Don't no one love Jim Limber." He pulled his ragged quilt to his chin. "I'll be good, Mama, and strong, just like you told me." Then Jim prayed. "My mama said I could talk to you anytime. I got lots of troubles. I wish you would help me."

The next day, Varina Davis and her children took a carriage into town to buy food. As they approached the general store, Maggie gasped, "Mama! Look!"

Across the street a man was beating a little boy. Varina stopped the carriage, sprang to the ground, and rushed over. "You stop hurting that boy!"

"He's my ward," the man said. "If I think he needs whuppin', I'm gonna whup him. Who do you think you are?"

A bystander shouted, "That's Mrs. Varina Davis, you fool! The First Lady of the Confederacy, the wife of Jefferson Davis!"

Varina snatched the man's strap and took Jim by the hand. "Young man, come with me." She led the sobbing Jim to their carriage and asked, "What's your name, child?"

"Jim Limber, ma'am."

"Children, say hello to Jim."

Maggie, Billy, Jeff, and Joe smiled and said, "Hello, Jim!"

"Are you going home with us?" Billy wanted to know.

"Where do you folks live?" Jim asked.

"We live in the White House," Joe said. "Come sit by me."

Jim hopped into the carriage and sat between Billy and Joe.

At the Davis home, Varina and her maid Ellen doctored Jim's cuts and bruises and fed him a good supper. Jim ate until he thought he would pop. After his supper, Ellen gave Jim a warm bath. Varina brought him some clean clothes. "Joe is close to your size and age, so these should fit you just fine, Jim."

Jim slipped on the bright yellow calico shirt, soft brown wool pants, and a jean-wool jacket. Hooking his thumbs into his suspenders, he strutted about the room like a proper Southern gentleman. Joe jumped up and strutted with him.

"My, don't you look nice, Jim. Now, you boys run and play," Varina said.

"Come on, Jim. I want to show you the White House!" Joe called.

Jim followed Joe through the house, laughing as they ran up the stairs and from room to room. They played hide-and-seek and then spun tops and whirligigs.

Later that night, Varina gathered the children together. "Children, it's story time. Tonight's story is about a farmer and his animals. Whomever I point to must imitate the sound of the animal I mention."

When Jim heard the Davis children mew, moo, whinny, oink, crow, and quack, he nearly fell out of his chair laughing. Of course, Jim made all the animal sounds too.

After she finished the story, Varina said, "It's bedtime, children, so say your prayers!" One by one she kissed them and wished each a good night's rest.

Jim knelt by his bed and thanked God for his rescue. "Please, God, let me stay here forever!"

At breakfast, Jim met President Davis. "I am pleased to meet you, Jim," Mr. Davis said. "And we have a surprise for you. We want you to live with us and be a part of our family."

"You mean I'll have another brother?" Joe asked. "Good! I don't want Jim ever to go back to that mean man. We're going to have lots of fun, Jim Limber Davis!"

At the Richmond mayor's office the next day, Jefferson Davis registered Jim as a free black child, listing himself and Varina Davis as Jim's legal guardians so no one could ever take him away.

Jim, Jeff, and Joe roamed Richmond's neighborhoods. They called themselves the Hill Cats. They played soldier games, hurling rocks at imaginary Yankees or staging mock battles with another group of boys who called themselves the Butcher Cats. Jim was such a fierce make-believe soldier that the boys called him "Hill Cat Jim."

When Christmas came, Jim Limber and the Davis family collected and repaired broken toys to give to the orphans at the Episcopalian Home. They also made cakes and candy and decorated the Christmas tree at Saint Paul's Church. Jim was so proud to have helped decorate the tree. On Christmas morning Jim was surprised to find homemade toys in his stocking. This was the happiest Christmas of Jim's life!

One day, Joe and Jim were playing together. Joe climbed up the iron gallery railing outside their house. He waved at Jim. "Look at me, Jim!" Jim laughed until he saw Joe slip and fall to the ground.

"Joe!" he cried. He rushed to Joe's side, but it was too late.

At Joe's funeral and burial, Jim wept with the Davis family. These were sad days for the Davis family, but especially for Jim because he loved Joe so much.

Later that month, Yankee raiders attacked Richmond. Mr. Davis rushed home to get his pistols. "Richmond is being attacked!"

They all knelt to pray for God's help, but Jeff and Jim soon jumped up. They wanted to help defend Richmond. Jeff said, "Please, Mother! Let's saddle my pony so Jim and I can go help Father fight the Yankees! We can pray later."

"If you boys go fight the Yankees, then who will protect me, Maggie, and little Piecake?" Varina questioned.

After the boys held a short conference, Jim said, "Don't worry, we boys will stay and protect you!"

The Yankee armies steadily marched closer and closer to Richmond. Mr. Davis decided to send Varina and the children south on a train so they could be safe. He promised to join them later.

The train was old and slow and could barely make it up the hills. One rainy night it broke down! They were stuck on the tracks in the darkness and rain far from any city. Jim, Jeff, and Billy took turns as sentries, making sure Mrs. Davis and the girls slept safely.

After soldiers repaired the train, they continued their journey. At Charlotte, the Davis family and a few soldiers left the train and traveled on to Georgia in a wagon.

One afternoon, several riders approached their camp. The men dismounted and walked toward the Davis campfire. The sentry cocked his rifle. "Who's there?"

"Jefferson Davis and my staff. I've come to rejoin my family!"

Jim watched Varina and the Davis children rush forward to embrace Jefferson Davis.

Mr. Davis held out his arm. "I need a hug from you too, Jim."

Jim ran to the strong arms of Jefferson Davis.

"Where are we going?" Jim asked.

"Texas, children. We're going to Texas."

Jim went to sleep that night excited about their journey to Texas. But the next morning, gunshots woke them and Yankee cavalry stormed into their camp. They put Jefferson Davis in chains and took him to an awful prison in Virginia. Mrs. Davis and the children were taken to Savannah and placed under house arrest.

When Savannah's citizens heard about the arrest of Jefferson Davis and the misfortune of the Davis family, they often walked by the house, encouraging Mrs. Davis and the children with words and gifts.

The Yankee guards were rude and mistreated the Davis family. Sometimes the soldiers stole money, clothes, and jewelry from their trunks and bags.

Captain Hudson was especially cruel to little Jim Limber, making fun of Jim and calling him a slave of Jefferson Davis. "I'm going to take that black boy away, and you'll never see him again!" he threatened.

"Jim is not a slave. He is free and a part of our family," Varina said. "You wouldn't dare take him."

Varina Davis was wrong.

The next night Captain Hudson and his guards broke into the house to take Jim away. Jim kicked and screamed and fought like a tiger, but the soldiers were too strong for him.

After the soldiers dragged Jim outside, the Davis children rushed to the door.

"The Yankees have kidnapped Jim Limber!" Billy shouted.

"Don't worry, Jim. We'll find you and get you back," Maggie said. "We love you, Jim Limber!"

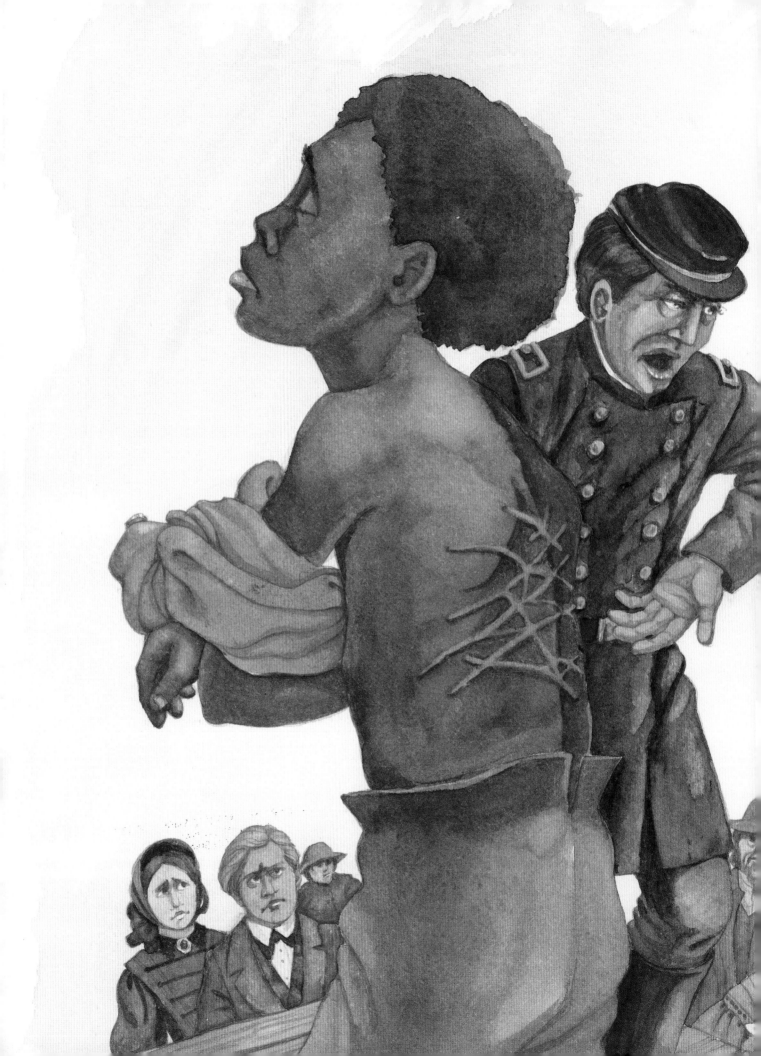

Captain Hudson took Jim north to Baltimore and Washington and displayed Jim to large crowds. He also made speeches about what a bad man Jefferson Davis was.

One night Captain Hudson pointed to Jim and said to the crowd, "This boy was a slave of Jefferson Davis. I want you to see how he has been mistreated. Jim, remove your shirt and show your scars."

Jim was afraid to disobey, so he took off his shirt. The crowd gasped when they saw the scars on Jim's back. Jim said, "My first guardian did this to me. Mr. Davis never beat or hurt me," but the crowd wouldn't listen. Jim was sad, and he didn't like the way people looked at him or the things they said about him.

A few in the audience did care for Jim. Several important black leaders were shocked at Jim Limber's treatment and demanded that it stop. After these men complained to the government, high-ranking officers ordered Captain Hudson to end these meetings and find a suitable guardian for Jim Limber. But Jim didn't want a new guardian. He wanted to go home to the Davis family.

Many months later, Jefferson Davis was finally released from prison. He was so happy to see his family.

"Where's little Jim?" he asked.

"The Yankees took him!" Varina said. "I am so worried. No one will tell me what they've done with him."

"We'll do all we can to find him," Mr. Davis said. He wrote people he knew in government positions and even sent letters to several newspapers. The letter he sent read:

I seek information on the health and safety of Jim Limber, a black orphan, about ten years of age. He was taken from my family by force in the summer of 1865. If you have any news of Jim Limber, please contact me.

Sincerely,
Jefferson Davis

After they mailed the letters, the Davis family knelt together and prayed that Jim Limber was safe and happy and that he would someday return home.

Epilogue to Parents

Jim Limber Davis's disappearance remains one of the great mysteries of the War Between the States. The Davis family searched for Jim for many years, but they never found him. Many scholars and historians have continued the search, but they too have failed to discover the fate of Jim Limber, a black orphan in the Confederate White House.